ADOBE PHOTOSHOP LIGHTROOM

ROWE THILLS

All rights reserved. No part of this publication may be reproduced, distributed, or transmitted in any form or by any means, including photocopying, recording, or other electronic or mechanical methods, without the prior written permission of the publisher, except in the case of brief quotations embodied in critical reviews and certain other noncommercial uses permitted by copyright law.

TABLE OF CONTENTS

What is Lightroom?....................8

THE LIGHTROOM CATALOG 11

    What's in a catalog? 12

    Best practices for working with Lightroom Classic catalogs 17

    Lightroom Collections 20

UNDERSTANDING THE DIFFERENCE BETWEEN PHOTOSHOP AND LIGHTROOM .22

    Similarities 24

    Difference #1: File Handling 27

    Difference #2: Editing Tools 31

Difference #3: Workflow 37

WHICH ONE IS RIGHT FOR YOU? 41

25 REASONS YOU SHOULD BE USING 43

1. Unlimited Undos 43

2. Slider-Based Controls 44

3. Sync Changes Across Multiple Images 44

4. Easy Publishing 45

5. Nondestructive Editing 45

6. Healing and Cloning 46

7. Easy Watermarking 46

8. Multitude of Presets 47

9. Work with Multiple Files 47

10. Before and After View 48

11. Built-in Google Maps for Geo-Tagging 48

12. Less Disk Space 49

13. Excellent Image Management 49

14. Strong Organizing 50

15. File Conversion.................... 50

16. Slideshow Display................ 51

17. Backup Feature 51

18. Better Printing.................... 52

19. Work from Multiple Computers 52

20. Lens Correction 53

21. Stress-Free Keywording 53

22. Easier to Use 54

23. Easy Photo Book Creation 55

24. Different Exporting Options... 55

25. Cheaper 56

ADOBE LIGHTROOM INTERFACE 57

Adobe Lightroom Creative Cloud Subscription 58

Lightroom Workflow and Tools 64

BEGINNER'S GUIDE TO LIGHTROOM **79**

The Importance of Adobe Camera Raw 80

Importing Photos 87

Organizing and Developing (Processing) 91

CONCLUSION **108**

What is Lightroom?

Lightroom is part Raw converter, part photo processor (yes, you can edit JPEG and TIFF files in Lightroom too), and part photo organizer. The latter task is often referred to as digital asset management (or DAM for short).

The key thing to understand about Lightroom is that it is a workflow application. It is designed to take care of your photos from the moment you copy them from your camera's memory card, to your computer's hard drive. Once in Lightroom you can process photos, add them to a map to show where they were taken, create a photo book or slide show, print them or export them to other programs for further processing.

This is why Lightroom is so useful, and so popular. It becomes the centre of your workflow, and while it is powerful enough to be used independently, it also integrates seamlessly with programs like Photoshop. You can use Lightroom by itself, or in partnership with other programs.

THE LIGHTROOM CATALOG

At the heart of Lightroom is the Catalog – a database that contains a preview of every photo that you have imported into the program, a record of each photo's metadata (including processing) plus the location where it is stored on your hard drive.

It is important to note that the Catalog doesn't contain the photos themselves, just information about them. Your photo files are always saved on a hard drive, even if you use Lightroom CC (Creative Cloud).

What's in a catalog?

A catalog is a database that stores a record for each of your photos. This record contains three key pieces of information about each photo:

- A reference to where the photo is on your system
- Instructions for how you want to process the photo
- Metadata, such as ratings and keywords that you apply to photos to help you find or organize them

When you import photos into Lightroom Classic, you create a link between the photo itself and the record of the photo in the catalog. Then, any work you perform on the photo — such as adding keywords or removing red eye — is stored in the photo's record in the catalog as additional metadata. When you're ready to share the photo outside Lightroom Classic — upload it to Facebook, print it, or create a slideshow, for example — Lightroom Classic applies your metadata changes, which are like photo-developing instructions, to a copy of the photo so that everyone can see them. Lightroom Classic never changes the actual photos captured by your camera. In this way, editing in Lightroom Classic is nondestructive. You can always return to the original, unedited photo.

The Lightroom Classic catalog versus a file browser

The way Lightroom Classic works is different from a file browser such as Adobe Bridge. File browsers need direct, physical access to the files they display. Files must actually be on your hard drive, or your computer must be connected to a storage media that contains the files, for Adobe Bridge to show them. Because Lightroom Classic uses a catalog to keep track of the photos, you can preview photos in Lightroom Classic whether they are physically on the same computer as the software.

The advantages of the catalog-based workflow

The Lightroom Classic catalog workflow provides two distinct advantages for photographers:

Your photos can be stored anywhere

Your edits are nondestructive

Lightroom Classic offers flexibility in managing, organizing, and editing photos because your photos can be anywhere — on the same computer with the Lightroom Classic application, on an external hard disk, or perhaps on a network drive. Because the catalog stores a preview of each photo, you can work with your photos in Lightroom Classic and see your editing changes as you work. And all the while, Lightroom Classic doesn't touch your original photo files.

Best practices for working with Lightroom Classic catalogs

It's wise to approach your work in Lightroom Classic with some forethought. You can move catalogs and photos, put photos in multiple catalogs, and combine or merge catalogs, but doing so can be confusing. In addition, links between your catalog and your photos may break. Follow these steps to plan your catalog setup and to minimize having to shuffle catalogs and photos around between computers and drives.

Decide in advance where you want to store your Lightroom Classic catalog. You can't store it on a network. You'll probably store it on your computer's hard drive or an external disk. After you decide where you'll save the catalog, consider the specific folder or path where you'll put it.

Determine where you want to keep your photos. How much disk space is on your hard drive? Will it be enough? If you're working on multiple computers, consider keeping your catalog and photos on an external drive that you can plug into either system. Copy or move your photos to that location before you import them into Lightroom Classic.

Finally, start Lightroom Classic and import photos into the catalog by adding them in place.

Lightroom Collections

One of Lightroom's key features is Collections. A Collection is like a virtual folder. You can call a Collection whatever you want, add as many photos as you like, and add photos to as many Collections as you need.

Using the above example, once you have imported your photos of Sarah into the Lightroom Catalog, you can add them to multiple Collections. For example, you may have one Collection that contains all your photos of Sarah, another with all your photos of London, and another with all the photos taken in July 2015.

It's a simplified example, but the advantages of Collections become more apparent the more you use them. In short, they give you the flexibility to organize your images in a way that suits you.

UNDERSTANDING THE DIFFERENCE BETWEEN PHOTOSHOP AND LIGHTROOM

One of the most common questions I hear from people just starting out in photography is, "What program should I use to edit my photos?". There are many free options such as iPhoto, Picasa, GIMP, and other commercial programs such as AfterShot Pro and Pixelmator but the most popular programs are Photoshop and Lightroom.

That question is usually followed by another, which seems quite logical, "What's the difference between Photoshop and Lightroom?". While the two programs do share many similarities, and are both widely used by the photographic community, they each serve a unique purpose and are quite different in some very major ways. Understanding what makes them similar, as well as different, can help you make an informed choice when selecting the right software for your needs.

Similarities

At the core level both programs do essentially the same thing, edit images. How they go about handling that task, as well as how you actually use each program, is quite different – but if you are simply looking for software that will allow you to alter, tweak, and enhance your photographs, either one will suffice. Both are capable of handling multiple file types such as: JPEG, PNG, TIFF, and a perennial favorite of many photographers, RAW. In fact both Photoshop and Lightroom use the

Adobe Camera Raw (ACR) processing engine to handle RAW files. So, you can expect similar controls and editing options in both programs when doing things like adjusting saturation, working with curves, and correcting for lens distortions.

Both programs also feature an extensive set of editing and manipulation tools allowing you to do everything from; basic edits like cropping and adjusting exposure, to advanced alterations such as working with brushes, tone curves, and graduated filters. You will find a variety of built-in effects in both programs that will allow you to instantly apply edits such as black and white, sepia, and other artistic styles. The two programs are quite powerful image editors. I know some photographers who use Lightroom exclusively and never touch Photoshop, as well as plenty of others who spend all day in Photoshop and never open Lightroom. However, in order to understand which one is best for you it might help to see how they are also quite different from each other.

Difference #1: File Handling

One of the most significant ways in which Lightroom is different from Photoshop is that it does not actually edit photos, nor does it move your images around to different locations on your computer. Instead all the changes you implement are kept in a separate file called the Catalog, which is sort of like a recipe book of instructions for how each photo should be processed. When you apply some type of edit, like a radial filter or adjustment brush, Lightroom is essentially keeping a log of the alterations in a database, while leaving the original image intact. It's a technique called nondestructive editing, which stands in stark contrast to how Photoshop operates.

Photoshop, on the other hand, operates quite differently. When you edit a picture such as a JPG, PNG, or RAW file in Photoshop you are always working on the original file itself, unless you save a copy as a

Photoshop PSD file that is usually several dozen megabytes in size. This PSD file contains all the changes made to a photo, and in order to share a given image it must then be saved to a final format such as JPG, PNG, etc. In essence, if you want to perform nondestructive edits in Photoshop you will end up with three separate files: the original camera RAW file, a PSD, and the final copy saved into a shareable format from the PSD.

The two processes look somewhat similar on the surface with one major difference; in Lightroom all your changes for every photo are saved in one single, relatively small, catalog file. In Photoshop all your changes are saved in unique files for every single picture you edit. This means much more space on your hard drive will be taken up as you work with multiple files in Photoshop, and you will end up with multiple versions of each image as well. So why would you want choose to use Photoshop instead of Lightroom? In a word, power.

Difference #2: Editing Tools

Lightroom is kind of like an all-terrain-vehicle you might see on some farms. It's fast, nimble, and can be used for a variety of tasks like hauling small objects and towing little trailers. But it simply cannot match the sheer power of a massive farm truck when it comes to getting big, serious jobs done like transporting massive bales of hay, pulling a horse trailer, or ploughing through mud and snow.

Nearly a decade ago Adobe realized that not everyone needed the capability of Photoshop, particularly photographers who were returning from events with hundreds of images to edit quickly. What this new generation of digital photographers demanded was the essential editing tools of Photoshop in one easy-to-use package which resulted in Lightroom.

Photoshop contains a dizzying array of filters, brushes, and other tools that allow you to perform all manner of edits and changes to your images. But more than that, Photoshop operates by letting you create different layers on which your edits actually take place. For example, the image on the right shows the various layers I used to edit the image of the statue, and each layer can be edited independently of the others. This might look like a lot, but it is not uncommon for a digital artist to use dozens of layers when editing an image. Lightroom, by contrast, works in a much more linear fashion with no layers, fewer editing tools and less overall flexibility. Both programs contain a history panel that lets you step back in time to any of your edits, but working with layers gives you infinitely more control over exactly how you edit your image.

Case in point, let's say you want to add a vignette to a portrait. In Lightroom it's as simple as clicking the "Vignette" option and changing a few basic parameters like the amount, how big the untouched middle portion should be, and how gradually the vignette should fade from the center. It's a quick no-fuss solution that is incredibly useful for all sorts of photography situations, and if you want a bit more control you can click on the Radial Filter for a few more options.

To do the same thing in Photoshop would require adding a special layer to your photo called an Adjustment Layer such as Levels. Then you'd adjust the levels to darken the image in the highlights and overall, and apply a mask to the layer to only darken the outer edges. You could also change the opacity of the layer (lightening the effect) or the Blend Mode, or you could apply a Dodge and Burn layer – and that's just the beginning. While all these additional steps might seem hopelessly convoluted, the more you learn how to use the tools Photoshop has to offer the greater degree of control you will have over the editing process.

With all of its options and features (including support for text, 3D graphics, and even video) Photoshop is ideal for almost any image-editing situation. Lightroom essentially distills Photoshop down to the tools that Photographers use most, which is one reason it is so appealing to many shutterbugs.

Difference #3: Workflow

Features and file options aside, the trump card that Lightroom has over its big brother involves its end-to-end workflow solution for photographers. Since it is designed specifically to address the needs of photography enthusiasts and professionals, it handles everything from importing photos from your memory card, to organizing, editing, sharing, and finally printing them. Lightroom has support for keywords and virtual folders to help you keep track of your images, and you can even use it to create a slideshow or photo book. Many photographers, even professionals, will go weeks or months without ever opening Photoshop, because Lightroom takes care of everything they need. On the other end of the spectrum is

Photoshop which doesn't transfer files, won't organize your images, and certainly can't make slide shows or photo books. But again, it's all about the tradeoffs you are willing to accept. Nothing else can even come close to Photoshop in terms of sheer editing power. However, you can use Adobe Bridge to handle some workflow-based tasks like importing photos and organizing the digital media on your computer, which when paired with Photoshop, does offer a more comprehensive Lightroom-esque workflow experience. It's not quite as streamlined as working in Lightroom alone, but it does provide a welcome degree of automation as opposed to manually organizing all your PSDs, JPGs, and other photos by hand.

WHICH ONE IS RIGHT FOR YOU?

By now you probably realize that this is a question only you can answer, and until recently it meant spending $150 on Lightroom or several times that amount on Photoshop. Thankfully, Adobe has made the decision much easier with its release of Creative Cloud and you can now get both programs for $10/month. If you don't like the idea of subscribing to software, you can still buy Lightroom by itself, and Adobe has stated they will continue to sell the standalone version for all future versions as well.

This book could be much, much longer and in many ways it seems like I have just scratched the surface, but I hope you have a better understanding of what makes these programs similar and different.

What about you? What differences do you think are worth noting between both programs, and what purpose does each serve for you? Leave your input in the comments section below.

25 REASONS YOU SHOULD BE USING

Lightroom for your photo editing needs.

1. Unlimited Undos

No matter how much you modify the original picture, Lightroom will keep a full history of all these actions even if you close the program. By contrast, Photoshop keeps track of the last 20 actions only, resetting its history when you close the program.

2. Slider-Based Controls

Whether you want to adjust brightness, clarity or any other such element, Lightroom offers slider-based controls that are very easy to use.

3. Sync Changes Across Multiple Images

Lightroom allows you to copy and paste changes across multiple images with just a few clicks – and it even asks you what changes you want to copy for faster image editing.

4. Easy Publishing

If you need to regularly publish images to your website, you can easily do this using Lightroom's "Publish Services." The program will export your picture(s) with the file name, at the dimensions, quality, and file format that you selected.

5. Nondestructive Editing

Unlike most other photo editing software, Adobe Lightroom does not edit original images, and instead imports a copy you can edit and later export as a different file.

6. Healing and Cloning

Thanks to Lightroom's healing and cloning features, you can easily remove blemishes, wrinkles and more to improve the quality of your pictures.

7. Easy Watermarking

Adding watermarks to your photos is extremely easy in Lightroom: you can either create a watermark using the program's function, or add your own photo as watermark and save it as predefined watermark.

8. Multitude of Presets

Lightroom uses presets instead of actions, which can dramatically modify the appearance of your pictures. You can create presets by making adjustments to a photo, or you can import them to the program.

9. Work with Multiple Files

Making changes to multiple images at the same time is possible in Lightroom – just select the desired pictures and start making adjustments.

10. Before and After View

One of the most valuable features of Lightroom is the "Before and After" feature, which enables you to compare the original and modified picture for easy reference throughout the editing process.

11. Built-in Google Maps for Geo-Tagging

Lightroom will automatically place your photos on the "Map" module if the camera you used to take them has GPS. You can even organize photos by location, which will oftentimes save you time.

12. Less Disk Space

Lightroom takes about 100MB of disk space, as compared to Photoshop's 1GB.

13. Excellent Image Management

Lightroom can easily create backup copies of your images in the desired file formats (e.g. raw for the catalog and DNG for archival copy), add keywords with very little effort, and apply presets with just a few clicks.

14. Strong Organizing

Adobe Lightroom has been specifically designed for photographers, so its organizing features are very strong. You can group images by camera type, ISO, date, and more, and you can also create collections based on specific criteria set by you. Once done, Lightroom will add any new imported pictures to the matching collection.

15. File Conversion

Lightroom supports most camera types, and it permits users to quickly convert between different file formats.

16. Slideshow Display

If you happen to run a studio, then you can make use of Lightroom's slideshow display, which plays your images with a variety of options, such as text labels, watermarks, and more.

17. Backup Feature

Lightroom is one of the few photo editing software to include a backup feature, which enables you to successfully back up your catalogs as often as you wish.

18. Better Printing

If printing is required, Lightroom can professionally handle it, providing tons of amazing printing options and page layout selections to achieve the best results.

19. Work from Multiple Computers

With Lightroom, you can successfully have a working catalog on a different computer for the times when you are on a shooting trip, and merge the images and metadata into your master catalog once you are back to your primary computer.

20. Lens Correction

Most notably, Lightroom enables users to correct any distortion and chromatic aberration produced by the lens. The program will read the EXIM data within your images, identify the type of lens that was utilized and at what focal length, and then proceeds to making corrections.

21. Stress-Free Keywording

Adding keywords to your images is critical to making them searchable.

Lightroom makes keywording extremely easy and stress-free, as you can add them individually to each photo, or add them to batches of pictures.

22. Easier to Use

While Photoshop is absolutely great for seasoned photographers and skilled graphic designs, it will be rather difficult to handle for beginners who want to learn photo editing the right way. Lightroom has a simple and well-structured interface that is intuitive and easy to use even for those with little or no experience.

23. Easy Photo Book Creation

Using the Book Module inside Lightroom creating photo books ready to go to print gets as easy as drag & drop!

24. Different Exporting Options

When you are done editing pictures, you have to export them – and Lightroom provides a very wide range of options. You can change file format, size, sharpen, embed profiles, burn to CD/DVD output, and more.

25. Cheaper

The last reason why Lightroom shines over Photoshop is price. The brand new Lightroom 6 can be purchased at about $149, while a standalone version of Photoshop costs over $699. The really awesome news though, is with Adobe's Creative Cloud photography plan you can get the most up to date versions of both Lightroom and Photoshop for only $9.99 a month!

ADOBE LIGHTROOM INTERFACE

It has been a long road of improvements since the first version of Lightroom, the most noticeable and important changes being in the tools between version 3 and 4 (with the change from the old-school "Fill Light" option to the current sliders for controlling Highlights, Whites, Shadows, and Blacks for illustrating being just one of the major adjustments accomplished).

With their mind on expanding their products to a broader market worldwide, Adobe now has two possible options for getting their software in your hands.

Adobe Lightroom: The lifetime-license version (which is actually the most expensive way of acquiring Lightroom even if updating it to new versions requires an 'upgrade fee'.)

Adobe Lightroom Creative Cloud Subscription

In 2012 Adobe launched a subscription system for every single application they offer, which also applies to Lightroom. The most popular package is the Adobe Creative Cloud Photography plan, which includes Adobe Photoshop CC and Lightroom desktop, mobile, and web. One of the benefits is that we can discontinue the service anytime we want without losing data in the process, although we won't be able to edit any new pictures without a valid license.

The major difference between these two versions is actually how often they get updated, Creative Cloud users often getting critical software updates before the Standalone users do. Lightroom's interface is split into panels and tabs. The tabs at the upper part define the environment module, with which we are working:

• Library: A catalog of our images and the main Module in Lightroom. It also offers a Quick Develop section that can be used with Presets installed in Lightroom.

• Develop: Lightroom's core module for making adjustments. This is the module where you can fully edit your pictures

- Map: Works with the Metadata information on your pictures, geotagging your pictures for easier location identification.

- Book: In connection with Blurb, Lightroom offers us access to a wide (paid) variety of templates, so we can use our photographs to create visually attractive books in PDF format

- Slideshow: Designed for creating videos and presentations inside Lightroom

- Print: In contrast to Adobe Photoshop, Lightroom takes into consideration all the variables needed for the printing process, developing its own print module for making this task easier for the user. Templates are provided (or you can design/buy new ones) for performing a layout design of our work before printing it.

- Web: This module, developed for use in combination with web design tools; creates web galleries with the pictures we processed inside Lightroom

In short, how you get the most out of Adobe Lightroom actually depends on your objective. For digital illustration needs, most likely you are going to use only the Library and Develop modules, but if you plan on using Lightroom strictly for all the print processes, then Lightroom actually provides enough tools, so you won't have to worry about acquiring new software like InDesign or Illustrator for doing a proper layout of your prints.

Lightroom Workflow and Tools

Beauty retouching can be handled with tools like Adjustment Brush, and Graduated/Radial Filters, with which you can apply modifications to certain areas with very precise parameters. Even if it may require further modifications inside Photoshop, it can be quickly combined with presets.

And as Lightroom's maid of honor, presets give us enough features that we could keep talking about them for days on end. You can work only with presets, which will require having a good preset library, or you can combine it with your photography optimization workflow.

Start by importing the pictures into the software itself. When you open up Lightroom, the software will take you inside the Library module. In case you have already imported pictures, the Library module will look like this

Workflow in Lightroom can be categorized according to the following options:

1. Photography optimization

2. Beauty retouching

3. Working with presets

This doesn't mean that you can't combine steps from one and another in order to create a beautiful work of art.

By Photography optimization, we are referring to getting the most of an image we shoot. This will depend mostly on the format of the image, since you, if you work with a JPEG file, are making adjustments to an already processed file, whereas you, if you use RAW as your preferred file format (please do this if your camera allows you to), have full control over the way the photograph will look, as RAW (just like the name implies) is a non-processed file format for digital photography.

In case you want to import pictures, go to the Import button on the left panel, and this new dialog box will appear

In this new window Lightroom will provide the options needed for importing our pictures, so we can be quite sure to label this as the first step inside our Lightroom workflow. Notice that unless you disable the option at the Preference menu, every time you insert a Memory Card, USB drive or CD/DVD disc, Lightroom will open at this very same screen, showing the options for importing media files.

Metadata can (if embedded on the file) also be accessed at the Library module. A preview of the image shooting conditions appears inside the Histogram panel with values related to ISO, Focal Length, Aperture, and Shutter Speed.

Now, switch to the Develop Module. The UI will change to match this change.

In the left inferior panel, Lightroom displays all the presets I have installed. A preview of our image is shown at the upper panel on the left side, which can be quite handy for previewing certain effects besides presets.

At the right side of the interface we see first the Histogram data, which, in addition to giving the information we mentioned before, also provides information regarding Blacks, Shadows, Exposure, Highlights, and Whites

Next, we have a number of tools displayed below the Histogram, which are as follows in order from left to right:

Crop tool: For cropping our image

Spot removal: Very similar to the Healing Spot tool inside Photoshop. You can sample a certain area, and then work your way through, applying corrections where needed

Red Eye correction: The name says it all – it is very quick for applying the needed correction

Graduated filter: Creates a gradient area where adjustments made, by you, are distributed according to their position in the gradient area

Radial filter: Works exactly the same way as Graduated Filter, but according to a radius rather than a gradient area

Adjustment brush: Works with exactly the same parameters as the previous tools, but allows you to apply the adjustments where needed

With these tools and the sliders in the panels below, you can create as many adjustments as you need. Take into consideration the next set of tips for enhancing your work within Lightroom:

Start by correcting the White Balance of the picture. This will define every other adjustment you can add later, such as color tint on the image. Always sample for neutral gray areas (which can be defined by having pretty similar values on R, G, B) or work your way with the sliders for a custom effect. Use the Exposure slider conservatively. The image tends to lose detail due to burning areas, so when you apply an increase with the Exposure slider you are only making things worse. If you compensate for your underexposure using highlights, whites, shadows, and black, you will end up with a much more professional looking outcome than by simply increasing exposure.

Increasing the values on sliders will depend on your objective. When we talk about increasing Whites and Highlights, this means going towards the positive values on the sliders. In case you want to increase Blacks and Shadows, go with negative values for those sliders, as positive ones actually decrease the amount of Blacks and Shadows present on the image.

Changes made on images are usually readily visible, and the most admirable feature of Lightroom is that the procedure works in a non-destructive way, meaning that the original image is preserved, even while we are able to change the values assigned to the image whenever we feel like doing so.

A quick way of creating more detail in the image is by increasing the Clarity slider, as it will add more light and detail to the image, but be careful as it can also add more noise as well.

Vibrance and Saturation sliders how Lightroom (like Photoshop) handles the amount of hue present in our images. Work with the Before/After, as this represents a quick and effective way of seeing modifications without having to export the image in order to compare it with the original file. Vignetting and Split Toning are always great finishes in every kind of situation. Learn your way around those effects, if you want to master Lightroom.

Presets inside Lightroom

Rather than requiring third party plugins, which will only slow down Lightroom performance, Presets are all the extra tools we need to achieve magnificent effects with our images. They can be defined as sets of instructions created around the parameters of native Lightroom tools for gaining a desired effect.

These elements allow us to change the conditions of a photograph quickly and can be used in combination with Lightroom's native tools, as well as by combining several presets made by different designers.

BEGINNER'S GUIDE TO LIGHTROOM

The Lightroom catalog is like a recipe book. Lightroom stores a record of all the changes you want to make to your images in a separate file called the Catalog, which is stored independent from your pictures. The best analogy I can think of is that of a kitchen: your original pictures are kind of like the raw ingredients in your cupboards, and the Lightroom Catalog is like a recipe book. Lightroom doesn't do anything to your ingredients (your original files), but instead saves the instructions for transforming your supplies into actual finished products (in this case output edited images), just like recipes for your photos. When you are finished, your original image files still remain, but you have a new creation (i.e. an edited picture) that you can share with others.

The Importance of Adobe Camera Raw

Before we get too deep into the weeds here, it's important to back up a bit and look at another program called Adobe Camera Raw (ACR), which allows you to perform all sorts of edits and changes to your Raw images – from simply making them brighter or darker, to selectively editing colors, or working with curves. You may already have it on your computer and not even know it, and it's actually the engine that powers everything Lightroom does in terms of editing your images. Every change, adjustment, and tweak you do to one of your photos in Lightroom, is actually being done by ACR.

Understanding how this fits in might seem a bit extraneous to the overall Lightroom discussion, but it's important to know how all it works together if you want to make sense of Lightroom itself.

Opening Lightroom for the First Time

When I initially launched my copy of Lightroom four years ago, things started to go south within a matter of seconds. It asked me about making a Catalog, and wanted to know where to store it, and I started channeling my inner Gob Bluth while muttering to myself, "I've made a huge mistake." If this sounds like you, don't worry – there's really not much going on here that you need to worry about, and everything will be fine. Remember the kitchen analogy I mentioned earlier? All your computer wants to know right now is where to store the Catalog, or recipe book, that it will use to keep track of the changes you want to make to your pictures. You will need to create a new Catalog, and specify its location on your hard drive. I just keep mine within my Pictures folder.

Some people are very specific about where they want this Catalog to be located, and professional photographers will often have multiple image collections and many catalogs as well. Honestly, if you just want to figure out how to use Lightroom you can just click the "Continue" button and go about your business. For casual photographers the exact location of the Catalog file is not all that important

In terms of new-user-confusion, the next screen (the Library module) you see is not much better. Upon encountering it for the first time I felt like someone had quashed my photography enthusiasm with a scary dull grey veil. There are a few tutorial hints that pop up in the middle, which aren't very helpful, and after you dismiss them you're left staring at an empty dark wasteland, wondering why you didn't just stick to using Instagram filters like everyone else.

What you're looking at here is your entire library of photos, but it's empty because none have actually been imported yet. There's plenty of other options and buttons here as well – enough to confuse even the most experienced user – so for now just ignore the Catalog/Folders/Collections stuff on the left side, and all those Quick Develop options on the right side. And for heaven's sake, don't give a second thought to those strange chessboard-like icons at the bottom. Just take a breath, grab your memory card and your favorite beverage, and get ready to import some photos. Plug your memory card into your computer, then click the

"Import" button in the lower-left corner to start transferring your pictures over to your hard drive. You can also import photos that are already sitting on your computer, but for now I want to focus on the kind of workflow you might encounter, as a photographer who just wants to figure out this program.

Importing Photos

The first thing you see once you have your memory card connected is a grid with tiny thumbnail previews of all the pictures on your memory card.

Note: You can also connect to your camera directly – however, it's a better idea to use a card reader then plug in your camera directly. If the camera battery dies during import you can crash the card and damage or lose your images.

There are all sorts of options on this screen, but if you just want to get the basics down, here's what you need to look at:

At the top of your screen, select the option that says "Copy." This will, as you may guess, copy the pictures over to your computer, and add them to the Lightroom catalog so you can make edits to them later.

On the right-hand side you have to choose a Destination so the program knows where to put the original photos on your computer. You can select a specific destination or just let Lightroom figure this out for you. You can also do things like rename your pictures as they are imported, apply specific edits (called "Develop Settings") to all of them, or give them keywords such as "Wedding" or

"Camping." For now don't worry about any of this, and I promise everything will be just fine.

Choose which pictures to import by making sure they have checkmarks in the top corner of each thumbnail preview. They should all be checked by default (if they aren't just click Check All), but if there are any images you don't want to import, you can just un-check the box next to them.

When you're all set, click the Import button in the lower-right corner of your screen. Your computer will beep or chime when everything is done, and you'll be ready to start editing your photos!

Organizing and Developing (Processing)

After your photos are imported things start to get really crazy, but once again just try to ignore all the new things that show up on the side of your screen, and focus on just a few of the essentials. First of all, don't start making edits or changes to your pictures just yet.

Instead, look at the left side of your screen and find an area called "Collections." Remember that Lightroom doesn't actually do anything with the original pictures. When you clicked Import, it copied them over to a folder on your hard drive where they will remain, intact and untouched, until the end of time. What you can do is organize the pictures into Collections within Lightroom itself, in order to keep track of them more easily. Collections function just like playlists in iTunes or Spotify, and allow you to sort photos manually or automatically, based on how you want them to fit together. Click the + button on the right side to make a new Collection (i.e. Playlist), Smart Collection (where sorts your photos automatically based on criteria you specify) or Collection Set (a folder containing multiple Collections). Once you have a Collection created you can populate it by dragging and dropping your photos over to it, just like in iTunes. During this process the original images stay exactly where they are on your hard drive, you are just using Collections to help manage them a little easier.

Once you have your images sorted into Collections it's time to start editing them. (Or you can start editing without doing any sorting at all. It's up to you.) Click the "Develop" option in the top-right corner of your screen to begin making changes (or click D on your keyboard). At first I was put off and confused by the term Develop, but Adobe used it to hearken back to the days of darkrooms and analog film photography. (which some photographers still use even today). Before digital cameras you had to actually get your film developed before you could see your pictures, and that's essentially what Lightroom is trying to emulate here in the Develop module. If it doesn't make sense to you yet, just pretend it says "Edit" instead of "Develop" and you'll be fine.

You are now in the Develop module, which is one of seven different working states available inside

Lightroom, the rest being: Library (which you started in), Map, Book, Slideshow, Print, and Map. I ignore all the others, and spend about 98% of my time in either Library or Develop, and as a new user I would recommend the same for you.

At first when you click on the Develop module it might not seem like anything is different, but look again and you will see that all the metadata information that was on the right-hand side of your screen has been replaced with a series of panels like

Basic, Tone Curve, Lens Corrections, and more.

One of the most basic edits many people do, is to trim them down so just the important parts are in the frame, and get rid of things along the edge like trees, trash cans, bystanders, and the like. To do this click the square icon under the colorful graph called the Histogram, (or use the keyboard shortcut R) and you will see a nifty overlay appear on your image that you can use to crop it down how you want.

Use the corners of the rectangle overlay to crop your picture down so it contains only what you want, then when you are done press the [enter] or [return] key to see the results. Remember what I said earlier about Lightroom being nondestructive? It might look like you have just removed part of your photo, but the original is entirely untouched, and remains fully intact on your computer. What you are actually editing here is a placeholder – a preview of what the final image will look like – not the actual image itself. None of your edits in Lightroom are permanent, and you can reverse or undo any editing decision you make, so don't be afraid to play around with it, kick the tires, and just start trying things even if you're not entirely sure what the result will be.

The other common edit that people make to their images is adjusting the brightness, often to fix an image that is too over or under-exposed. This can easily be done with the top panel on the right side of the Develop module, appropriately titled "Basic."

Look for the slider called "Exposure" and move it to the right or left in order to make your picture brighter or darker.

Once again you will notice the changes you make reflected on the picture you see, but keep in mind you are not actually editing the original photo. Your instructions to crop, brighten, or otherwise change the picture are being stored in the Catalog file, while the original remains untouched. At this point you can go ahead and experiment with all the other options, tools, and sliders you see in the Develop module and take note of how they alter your photo. Even if you are not at all sure of what is happening just remember that Lightroom is nondestructive so you may as well play around with things to your heart's content, since your original pictures will never be altered, and are safe.

Exporting (Save As)

Once you have made all the changes to a picture that you want, it's time to export the final photo. This is again where the cooking analogy may come in handy, since this step is similar to putting your cake, casserole, or quiche, in the oven so it can bake. You still have the original ingredients on your counter and in your pantry, but once your timer beeps you will have an entirely new creation based on the recipe you used.

In Lightroom you edit photos instead of making pastries or pies, and the Export step is when you put them in your virtual oven to be processed. You may also think of this as opening up a document or spreadsheet, making some changes, and then choosing "Save As" instead of "Save." This leaves the original document intact while creating a new one with your changes, much like exporting a picture in Lightroom leaves your original image as it was, and gives you a new edited version, complete with all the edits you made.

When you are ready to export a photo or multiple photos, select the ones you want while in the Library or Develop module and choose "File >

Export", which will bring up yet another confusing dialog box filled with head-spinning options and choices. Hopefully by now you are getting a little more used to this sort of thing when using Lightroom, but if not just focus on a few specific items on this screen.

On the left side you will see a few presets for exporting your photos, depending on whether you want to print them, email them, etc. You can also create your own presets for exporting, but for now don't worry about that and just focus on a few specific settings.

If you're not sure which option to choose, start with "Full-Sized JPEGs" and then modify things just a bit by tweaking a couple settings (make sure Export To: is set to Hard Drive at the top of the box). Then find and adjust the following:

File Settings – Choose "JPEG" as the Image Format, set the quality slider to 85, and Color Space to sRGB.

Image Sizing – Tick off "Resize to Fit" then choose "Width & Height" and then enter 2048 in both the W (Width) and H (Height) boxes, (make sure it says "Pixels after Height, not In or Cm.). Leave the rest of the parameters alone.

Post-Processing – make sure After Export is set to: Show in Finder (or Show in Windows Explorer if you use a PC).

These settings will give you pictures that are large enough to print up to about 5×7" size, or share on social media sites, (for email use a slightly smaller size like 1200 or 800px).

When you're ready, click the "Export" button in the lower right corner and you're all set. As long as you did the last part, Lightroom will open a Finder (or Windows Explorer) window showing you all your new images, and where they are on your harddrive. Lightroom will probably save the edited copies of your pictures to your Desktop (the default) but you can double check this using the "Export Location" option (at the top of the box) in the Export pop-up box if you want.

CONCLUSION

Finally, Adobe Lightroom is an amazingly developed software for photographers and image editors. While Photoshop is a more complex program to use for image editing, Lightroom is a straightforward and simple software mostly used by beginners and freshers.

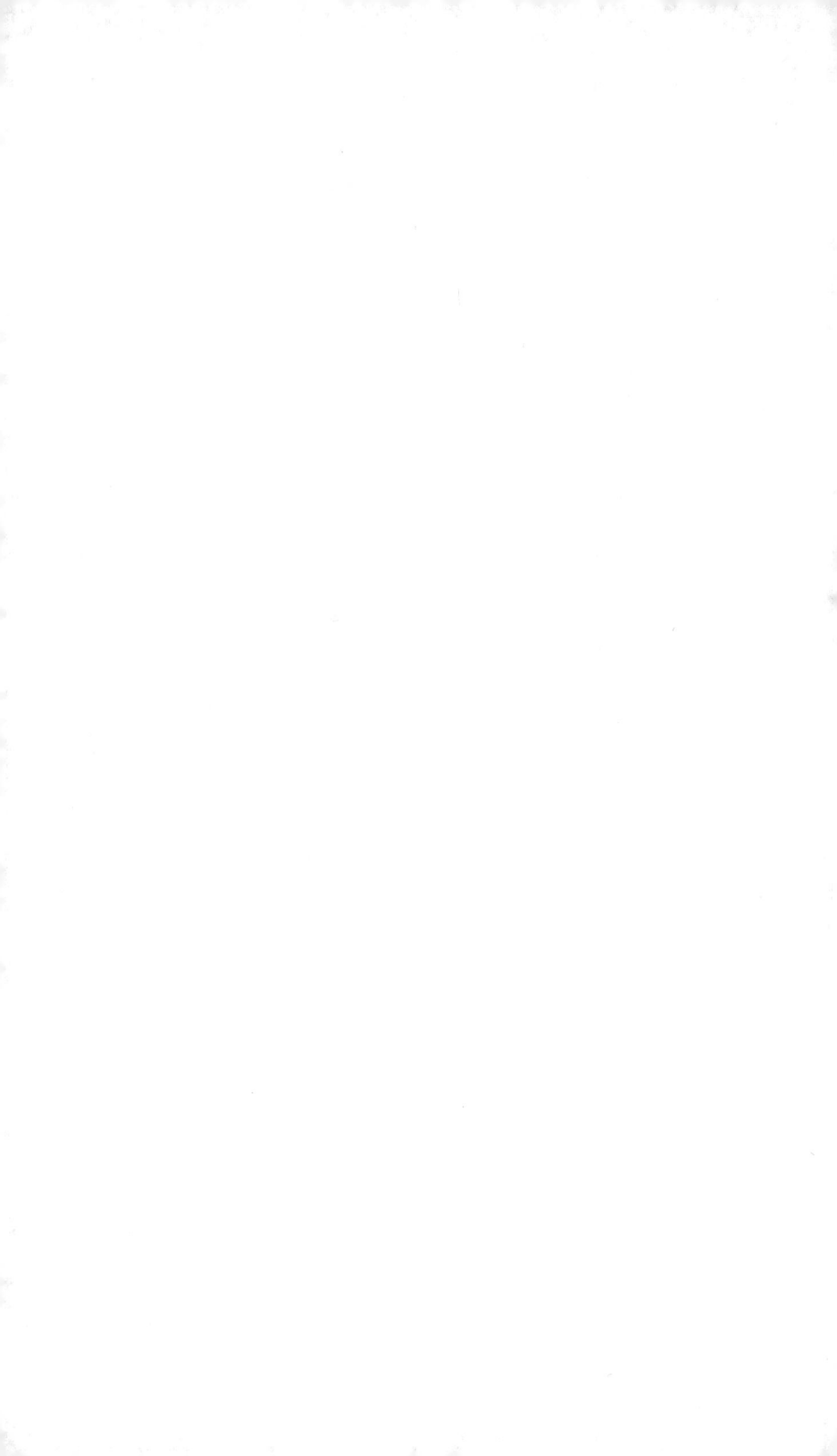

www.ingramcontent.com/pod-product-compliance
Lightning Source LLC
Chambersburg PA
CBHW070243220526
45465CB00004B/1505